T0380868

The
NIGERIA
I Know

JENNIFER MOLLENHAUER

The
NIGERIA
I Know

JENNIFER MOLLENHAUER

To my mother, Elisabeth Wickham Fitzhugh, who showed me how to love books. - Jennifer Mollenhauer

In loving memory of my father, Peter Dixon Nnajiofor Ogbodo, who is never far from my thoughts. - Royce Dixon

Royce: Hi, you beautiful! You single?

Jennifer: Thank you! No, I'm a happily married woman.

Royce: Hi fam woman.

Jennifer: Hi, where are you from?

Royce: Nigeria.

Jennifer: That is a long way from here in America.

Royce: Yea, but I wish people didn't see us as bad.

Jennifer: What do you mean?

Royce: They think we are uncivilized or all living in a jungle.

Jennifer: Ok.

Royce: I've never even seen a jungle.

Royce: I want people to know the Nigeria I know.

WHAT HAVE I DONE?

I have done everything I was taught not to do. I have talked to a stranger. I have told him about my life and me. And because I have done this, I have learned something of a place that was only a name to me. Now, I read about it in the news and look at the photos with some familiarity. Nigeria is still a foreign land to me that I find somewhat frustrating and bustling. But now that I have a friend there, I am trying to understand it and memorize the details. I am more aware, now. I didn't realize that I wasn't aware before.

My purpose in writing this book is to share that awareness. I believe it is worth a look. I see the dry, dusty climate as the backdrop for these people who crave security and dignity. They go through their days commuting, making things, or buying food. This book was written as a new president was elected, in Nigeria. The people hope for better times ahead. From the photos offered, you can see that times are hard and positive change is something the people could really use. This is a land of dust and dirt, where people range from ragged to wealthy. In the news about Nigeria there is violence, but people go about their lives everyday. This is what it looks like from where Royce stands. The photos were all taken with his cell phone.

I began the written part of this book after meeting Royce only six weeks before. I met this man on Instagram and nearly all of our conversations have been on Whatsapp. We have a social media friendship. We are people in different economic and educational situations, yet we have been real with each other. At times, we have laughed and joked about things. At times, we have fought and misunderstood each other. From our various correspondences, I have taken sections of our conversations that relate to the photos I was given. There is simplicity in the cadence of his texts that to me is so poetic and striking. I wonder if you, as the reader, can see that, too?

As you look through this book, I ask you to see this place and the people that were once completely foreign to me. I asked Royce, "What do you want to show in this book?" He answered, "You know the game - the good and the bad." I thought of this as I looked back at the photos he had taken. It struck me! He was right! In nearly every photo it is there - the good and the bad.

WATERFRONT

Jennifer: Where in Nigeria do you live?

Royce: Lagos.

Jennifer: Wait- let me look it up on a map.

Jennifer: Lagos is by the water.

Royce: Yes, we have many beaches.

Jennifer: I like beaches. Do you ever swim in the ocean?

Royce: NEVER.

Jennifer: Really, why not?

Royce: I can't really swim.

6

WATERFRONT

Jennifer: Have you ever gone boating?

Royce: Yes.

Jennifer: When was the last time?

Royce: Maybe a couple of years ago.

Royce: My friend has a yacht.

FOOD

Jennifer: What do you buy for food?

Royce: Rice, noodles, beef, chicken.

Jennifer: Do you eat fruit?

Royce: Yea, bananas, plantains, yams, different kinds of mangos.

Jennifer: There's more than one kind of mango?

Royce: Yea.

Jennifer: I didn't know there was more than one kind of mango.

FOOD

Jennifer: Can you tell me about the white puffy thing in two of the pictures? My husband said he thought it was called foo-foo?

Royce: LOL.

Royce: He's right.

Royce: But it's spelled fufu.

Jennifer: What's it made of?

Royce: It's made of cassava.

Jennifer: I've never heard of that.

Royce: You use that [fufu] to take soups. You dip it in the soup.

Royce: It's African food.

Jennifer: Ok.

Royce: For the Ibo.

Jennifer: Special to your culture?

Royce: Yea.

Royce: Yoruba native meal is amala and ewedu.

FOOD

Jennifer: Was this from the market?

Royce: No, this is a food stand in my neighborhood.

Royce: This is Jollof rice with sweet potato and vegetables.

FOOD

Jennifer: What are you having for dinner?

Royce: A loaf of bread and tea.

FOOD

Jennifer: What are you making for dinner?

Royce: Yams in a sauce.

Jennifer: Do you like to cook?

Royce: Love to cook! I'm a good cook! I'll cook for you someday.

TRANSPORTATION

Jennifer: Can you tell me about the airplane?

Royce: I'm standing in line to board the plane.

Jennifer: Where were you going?

Royce: I was going to Lagos from my home state of Enugu.

Jennifer: What side of the road do you drive on? Right side like us?

Royce: Same as America.

TRANSPORTATION

Jennifer: What are the things that look like yellow buses?

Royce: Buses.

Jennifer: Oh, right.

Royce: We have what you have.

Jennifer: Yes, but it is still a bit different.

TRANSPORTATION

Royce: The bike riders are what we call OKADA.

Royce: That's also a means of transportation.

TRANSPORTATION

Royce: People [are] going to work.

Royce: Bus fares increased and most of them are stranded.

Royce: No fuel.

Royce: I was stranded like that today.

Jennifer: That's amazing⋯ Is your new president saying he'll do something about it?

Royce: He [the president] can't do anything. There is a petroleum minister.

Jennifer: I read that Nigeria was a fuel producer for other countries. So, why is it so scarce? You might not know these answers. I was just curious.

Royce: LOL, I got fuel for N240 per litre, last night.

Royce: We have oil. We export oil to refine. Then import it back.

ON THE ROAD

Jennifer: What are they selling at the stopped cars?

Royce: They sell anything.

Royce: Car phone chargers.

Royce: Drinks.

Royce: Water.

Royce: Fruits.

Royce: Everything.

ON THE ROAD

Royce: It's hard here.

Royce: Sometime we live from hand to mouth.

Royce: When we get food we put it in our mouths.

Royce: It doesn't even make it to the table.

Royce: You get?

WEALTH

Royce: There is money here, too.

Jennifer: Are there skyscrapers?

Royce: Yea, and nice buildings behind gates.

Royce: I can't go in. The guard won't even let me look through the bars.

Royce: I stopped to look. He told me to move on.

WEALTH

Jennifer: I've never heard of someone named Royce before.

Royce: You haven't? It means royal.

Jennifer: No, no one I know has that name except you.

Royce: Haven't you heard of the car, Rolls Royce?

Jennifer: Haha - yes, I have heard of that!

MONEY

Jennifer: I am a biologist and I have a belly dance studio. I lead nature hikes and teach dance classes all the time. Do you have a job?

Royce: Not anymore. I'm in Politics. I was a Personal Assistant during the election campaigns. The campaigns are over.

Jennifer: It's not a year-round job?

Royce: No, there's no job security here.

Jennifer: Can you get another job?

Royce: There was another job, but it was too far away. I couldn't afford to get there.

Jennifer: I'm sorry.

Royce: It's Ok.

MONEY

Royce: It's hard to find jobs. Even people with university degrees can't find work. You get?

Jennifer: Yes.

Royce: When you do get work it doesn't pay enough. When you buy food and pay the bills, it's gone and it wasn't even enough.

Jennifer: I'm sorry.

Royce: What'd you doing?

Jennifer: We [my family] are at the ballet production of Peter Pan. It's about to start.

Royce: Not bad.

Jennifer: I like going to the theatre and museums. That's how I like to have fun.

Royce: Hmm, it's good you're not a Nigerian woman.

MONEY

Jennifer: I saw you had a peaceful turn over for the first time in history, with your new president.

Royce: Yea, I was worried about war.

Jennifer: I know. I read that they both threatened war if they didn't win.

Royce: Maybe the change will be good. We could use some hope.

Jennifer: Will there be more jobs?

Royce: This is what he says:
1. Stabilize oil prices at $100 a barrel.
2. To reduce fuel price to N45 a litre.
3. Provide free education to all Nigerian children.
4. Pay the poorest 25 million people N5000 every month.
5. Generate 40,000 megawatts of electricity in 4 years.
6. Pay youth corps for one more year after service.
7. Provide one meal a day for all Nigerian students.
8. Provide 3 million jobs in his first year.
9. To make N1 to be equal to $1.
10. Build 4 refineries in 4 years.

Royce: Hmmm.

Jennifer: That is a lot to promise. We will see what happens.

Jennifer: I hope it doesn't take too long.

Royce: Yea.

MONEY

Royce: This is a Kindergarten.

Jennifer: I like the colors on the building.

Royce: I went to private schools.

Royce: Then, I did some courses at the Uni.

Jennifer: Do you mean College?

Royce: University, but I didn't finish.

Royce: I want to go back, but - you know.

WEDDINGS

Royce: When I get married, I'll make sure your daughter is in the bridal train.

Jennifer: Thank you.

Royce: She will walk barefoot. And she will carry a basket with something in it.

Jennifer: That would be different for her.

Royce: She would walk around my in-law's family. Using me here- I'd take one of whatever is in the basket [out] and replace it with any amount of money.

Jennifer: Does she keep it?

Royce: She keeps the money. It's hers.

Jennifer: Wow.

Royce: That's [how it was] for my brother and wife's wedding.

Royce: Not everyone has a traditional wedding.

WEDDINGS

Royce: We have different traditions.

Royce: We have what we call aso ebi.

Royce: The bride and her family will buy cloths.

Jennifer: Ok.

Royce: Then they cut the cloths in pieces and sell to people to go sew them and wear to the wedding.

Jennifer: Do they sew a piece on the inside of their outfit or can it be seen?

Royce: No, it's not rags. They buy yards to make clothes. You know yards?

Jennifer: Oh, like buying bolts of cloth.

Royce: I guess so.

Royce: You'd see us all wearing them [like] uniforms.

Royce: That's the aso ebi.

PEOPLE

Jennifer: Are you Ibo?

Royce: I'm Ibo.

Jennifer: What makes a person Ibo?

Royce: It's tribes.

Royce: Three major tribes: Ibo, Yoruba and Hausa.

Jennifer: Oh, see I'm learning all the time.

PEOPLE

Jennifer: You mentioned you have Ijaw in your family.

Jennifer: Ijaw is what tribe?

Royce: No, Ijaw is part of the Niger Delta.

Royce: They live in water.

Jennifer: Such a different world! Ugh!

Jennifer: How do people live in water?

Royce: Yea.

Royce: Ijaws are mainly fishermen.

Royce: They build wooden houses on water.

Royce: Google Maroko Slum... It's similar.

Jennifer: Wow, that's so fascinating!

Royce: Sad right?

Jennifer: No!

Royce: Haha.

Jennifer: Interesting! In a crowded world, to make the water work for you is amazing!

Royce: True.

PEOPLE

Jennifer: She is beautiful. Who is she?

Royce: A tailor.

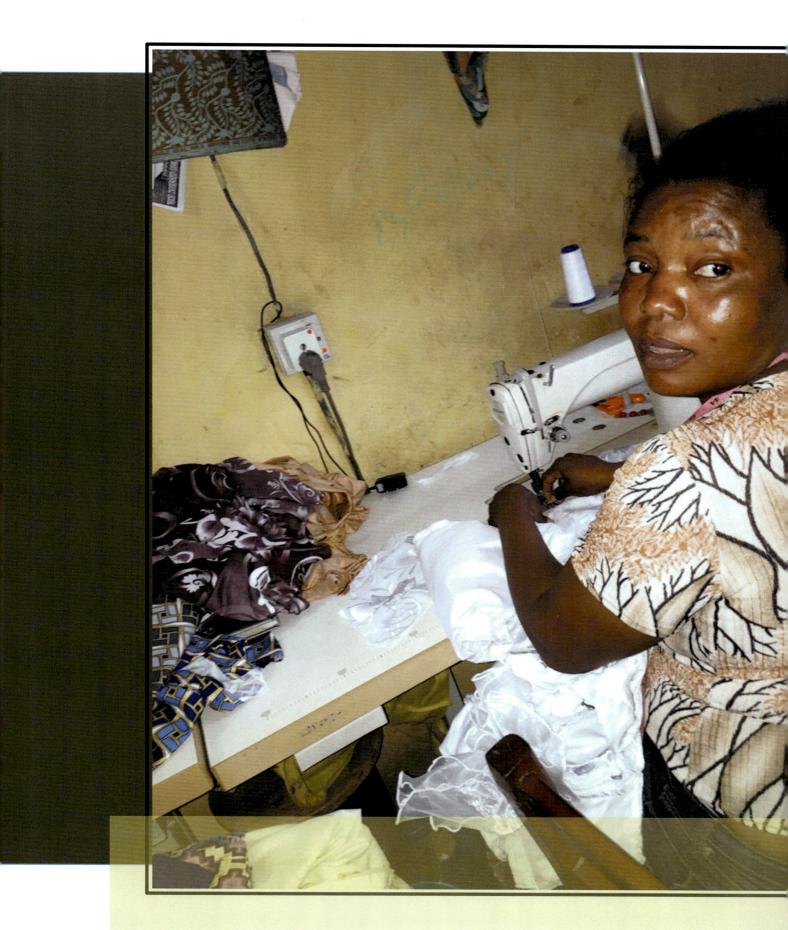

PEOPLE

Jennifer: Do you know the boy with the bag?

Royce: No, he's just in my neighborhood.

PEOPLE

Jennifer: That is a wonderful picture.

Royce: Yea, my man in the wooden shop.

Jennifer: There is so much being said in that picture.

Royce: Ok.

THE MALL

Jennifer: I don't have an idea of how you buy clothes and things.

Royce: We have malls and we have markets.

THE MARKET

Jennifer: What do they sell there?

Royce: Everything. You know food, clothes, house things.

Jennifer: It looks crowded.

Royce: It's always busy.

THE MARKET

Royce: The men with wheelbarrows help carry people's stuff.

Jennifer: Do they get paid for that?

Royce: Yea, like half a dollar.

CHURCH

Jennifer: Do you know that I am Jewish?

Royce: O yea?

Jennifer: I assume you are Christian.

Royce: Catholic.

Jennifer: Ok.

Jennifer: I am ready to do the written part of the book.

Royce: God Guide Us.

THIS IS WHAT I'VE DONE!

Perhaps you can see what an extraordinary thing has happened. I have learned so much about a place that not long ago was a name, Nigeria, somewhere in Africa. Now, not only can I find it on a map, I know where different tribes hail from. I know what the people and buildings look like and that Lagos is beside the Gulf of Guinea. And through the photos that Royce has given me, I will never forget the color of the dry dirt that is different to me, though so prevalent there.

Royce and I began in our friendship with small amounts of superficial information about our cultures. Knowing about transportation options and what is at a market is just the beginning of what is really going on in a place. That was evident when I asked the deeper question of what the man with the wheel barrel was paid for his efforts, while waiting to be hired and walking in the hot sun. Over time, Royce began letting me know far more intricate details about his culture. This grew as our trust in each other grew. By the time I am writing this last section of the book, I have known Royce for only two months. Of course, in two months time I do not know everything there is to know about Nigeria. I'm sure there are nuances I can never quite understand, because I did not grow up in that culture. But what I have gleaned is very interesting to me.

The title of this book can be viewed differently by the end of the reading exploration. In the beginning, this project was all about what Royce knew of Nigeria. He wished to share with me, and through me with you, the Nigeria he knew. However, what I have presented to you is really what I now know of Nigeria. It is the knowledge that I have gained over the past two months that you are truly seeing. And so in the end the title has evolved to have a double meaning.

I have also gained a sense of perspective on cultural misconceptions. I had and still have misconceptions about what is normal to Royce, in Nigeria. He has misconceptions about what is normal to me, here in America. Although, I am proud to say, we are closer to an understanding than when we first met. We have even had some awkwardness that was simply due to using the English language differently. Nigerians generally learn English, because the British once occupied Nigeria.

When we first started texting each other, I sent Royce a photo of my house thinking he would find it nice and interesting (I hoped even beautiful). His response was to text, "Not bad." In my American cultural experience "Not bad" is a sarcastic and often hurtful comment. I didn't mention my hurt and just continued with our conversations. It soon became clear that he meant it as it was written. He meant it was really not bad and in fact good.   In my turn, I confounded him one day when I had a bad headache and I said, "It was a real treat." His response was, "Really?" Even with the bad headache, I had to laugh at myself. I told him, "No, that I was joking." I really was learning something about how sarcastic Americans are and that other cultures might not understand our seemingly constant levity.

So, throughout these past two months of learning about Nigeria and Royce, I was also learning about myself. This relationship made me further aware of how much plastic packaging I was getting from the grocery store and then throwing into the trash and recycle bins. I was thinking that people in Nigeria would probably look at these perfectly good containers that once held margarine, cottage cheese or hummus and wonder at us having so many dishes that it wasn't practical to keep them.   So, we Americans throw them away. Royce sent me many more photos than what I chose to put in the book. Some were not in focus and some were simply repetitive. In a few market photos, people were selling what looked like used shoes. I suppose that if these containers could be sent over to Nigeria, someone might try to sell what I was simply throwing away. My trash might be a valuable source of income.

I was also struck by what, at first, I perceived as him being wasteful. Royce told me one day, when I let him know I was washing my laundry, that he sent all of his laundry to the cleaners.   At the time, I thought that it was a waste of money to send laundry to someone else. I didn't tell him I was thinking this and in fact reading it here will be his first knowledge of it.   But as I considered it longer, I became more aware of what I was doing. It costs a large amount of money, up-front, to own a washer and dryer. It takes a large amount of water to run the washer and electric and gas consumption to heat the water and dry the clothes. Is it truly cheaper or just more convenient for me to have the laundry machine in my house? I don't actually know the answer, but the question does make me think about the energy I am consuming while carrying out the act of doing my laundry.

I pause to look out over my beautiful spring garden. I have planted flowers and trees to make me happy and give the wildlife at my suburban home food and shelter.   I once asked Royce, "When do your flowers bloom?" He said, "We don't really grow flowers here. That's not something people

care about in this neighborhood." I feel very fortunate to live in a climate with four seasons and a country where the government has passed human rights laws such as minimum wage for workers, health care benefits, and social services for those who are in need. I still very much love my American culture. I have also really enjoyed learning about Nigeria, though it has been sometimes startling and heartbreaking. I am pleased that I am more aware. I am an educated, well read, and inquisitive person. However, I had been selective about what I was learning. My meeting Royce, this social media friendship, has made me grow in a direction I didn't know was lacking. I am forever grateful to him for this gift. And we have made a book together without ever meeting in person. We have done this from across the world! Just two months ago we were strangers. We are not strangers anymore.

Printed in the United States
By Bookmasters